The James Webb Space Telescope: The History of the Most Powerful Telescope in Space

By Charles River Editors

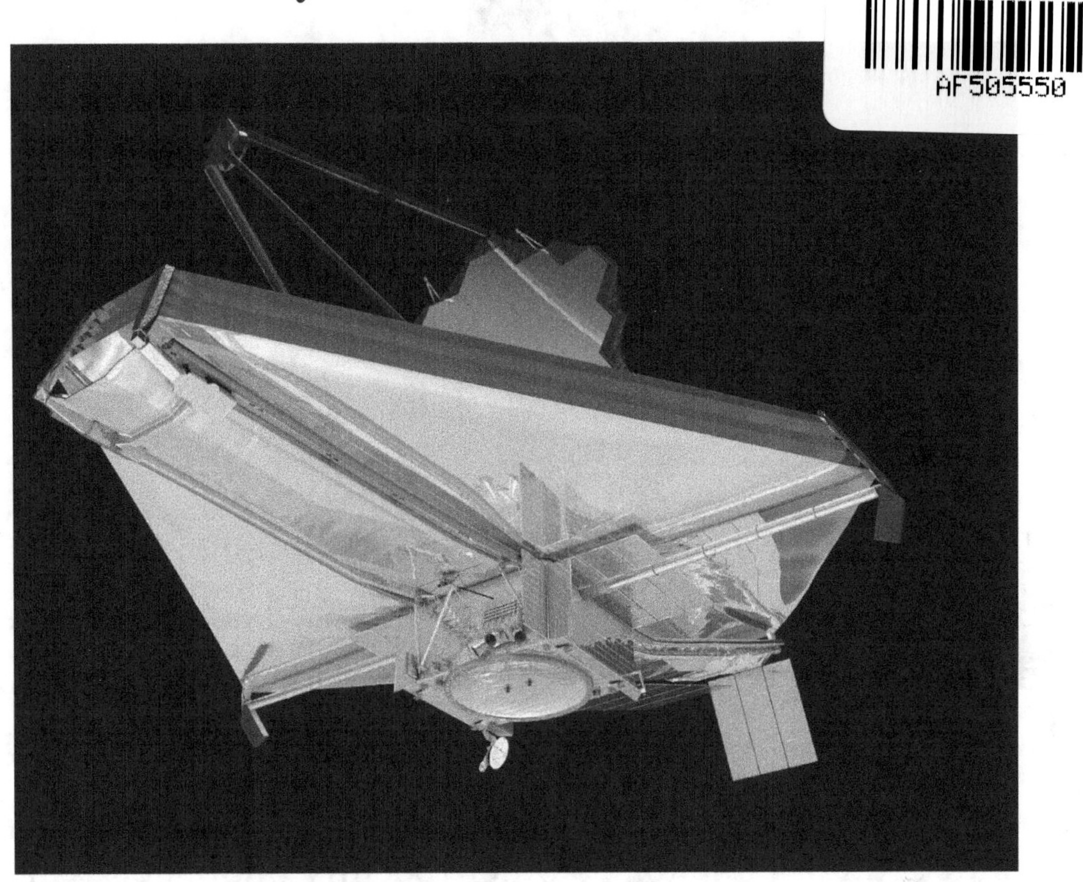

A picture depicting the underside of the telescope

About Charles River Editors

Charles River Editors is a boutique digital publishing company, specializing in bringing history back to life with educational and engaging books on a wide range of topics. Keep up to date with our new and free offerings with this 5 second sign up on our weekly mailing list, and visit Our Kindle Author Page to see other recently published Kindle titles.

We make these books for you and always want to know our readers' opinions, so we encourage you to leave reviews and look forward to publishing new and exciting titles each week.

Introduction

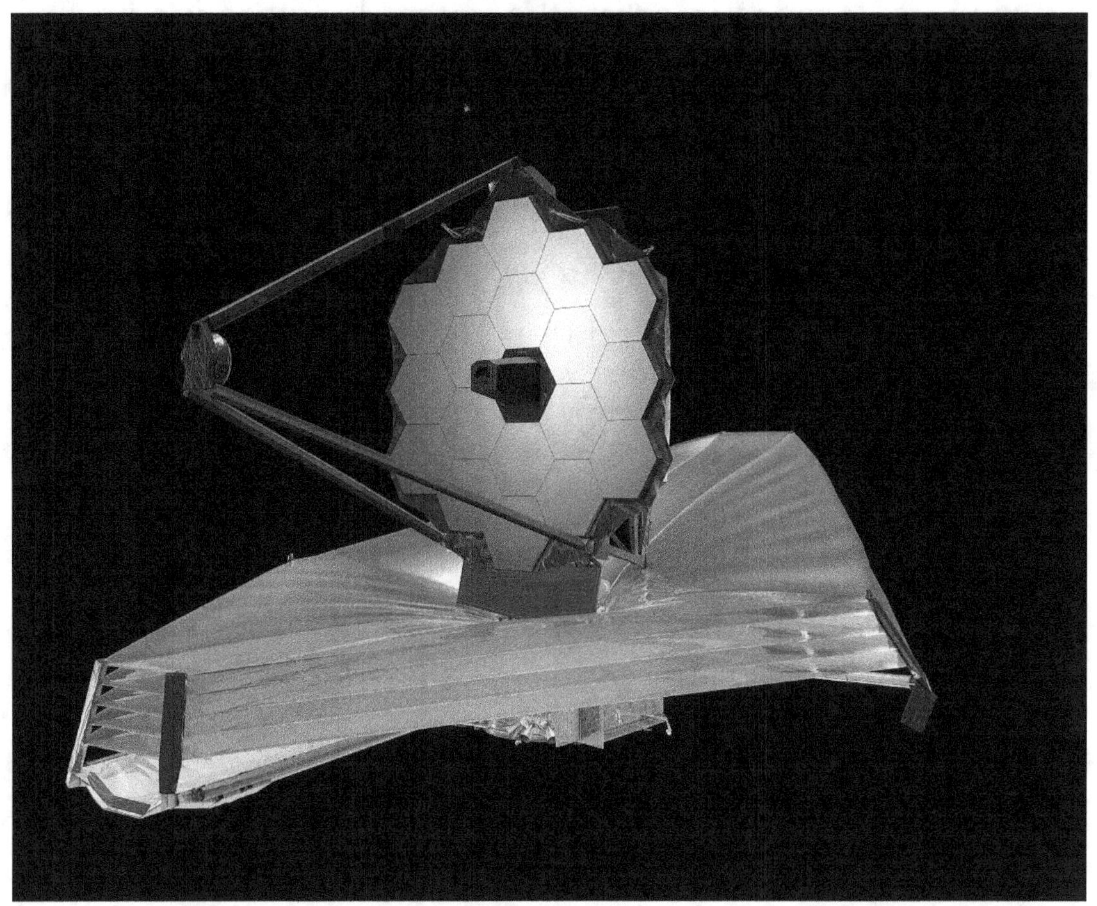

A picture depicting the top of the telescope

On April 24, 1990, the Space Shuttle *Discovery* lifted off from Kennedy Space Center on the Space Shuttle Program's 35th mission, but this was no ordinary mission. In its payload bay, *Discovery* was carrying the Hubble Space Telescope, with the objective of putting the telescope into orbit.

Despite the costs and initial defects, the Hubble telescope has been a remarkably successful project, furthering astronomers' understanding of the universe more than any other telescope or instrument in history. During its decades in orbit, the versatile telescope has taken high resolution images of objects billions of light years away, giving astronomers a look at the early universe. Along the way it has also taken the most detailed pictures of the solar system, captured the most striking images of star creation and supernovae, and uncovered evidence of phenomena like gamma-ray bursts and dark energy.

What made Hubble so crucial is that by escaping Earth's atmosphere, the telescope's views eliminated limitations and interruptions that are a natural part of land-based telescopes. Land-based telescopes are larger, cheaper, and easier to maintain. They are also not vulnerable to the risk of colliding with space junk or fast-moving small meteoric materials. However, even at 11,000 feet, ground-based installations have historically faced atmospheric distortion. The atmosphere blurs the light when a picture is taken through it, and since the 1960s, science has increasingly leaned toward space-based instruments, at first attaching them to balloons and sending them aloft to "carry them above Earth's lower atmosphere."[1]

The atmospheric distortion problem with ground telescopes has been largely ameliorated in recent years by

---

[1] Space Versus Ground Telescopes, June 7, 2016, University of Arizona – www.research.arizona.edu/stories/space-versus-ground-telescopes

the development of "adaptive optics."[2] A ground-based facility can now produce an image as sharp as that of a space telescope. This makes the division of labor between the two a bit clearer. The space instrument provides a wider field of view in addition to fine optical resolution, and it is no longer necessary to use "visual to near-visual"[3] telescopes operating in space. In fact, optical telescope photos are available in high quality for the general public based on NASA technology. Boston Micromachines claims to provide "clearer pictures of celestial objects in deep space than ever before…with 'deformable' mirrors that compensate for atmospheric disturbances and instrument misalignments."[4]

Still, scientists need to build space telescopes, not just for high resolution pictures but also to work in wavelengths one cannot observe from Earth. From space, telescopes that work in parts of the non-visual wavelengths provide the only means of viewing x-rays, gamma rays, and extreme ultraviolet rays. Most importantly, they provide "excellent platforms for observing in the far-infrared"[5] spectrum.

The Hubble telescope, working in space less than 400

---

[2] Quora, Pros and Cons of Earth-Based Telescopes vs. Space Telescopes – www.quora.com/What-are-the-pros-and-cons-of-the-Earth-based-telescopes-vs-space-telescopes

[3] Quora

[4] Boston Micromachines Corporation, Perform at a Higher Level with the Latest Technology – www.bostonmicromachines.com/deformablemirror-applications/astronomy/

[5] Quora

miles above the Earth's surface, produced photos of galaxies previously unseen as they existed only 500 million years before the "Big Bang." It was fortuitous that Hubble outlived its anticipated lifespan by many years, because the launch of its successor, the James Webb Space Telescope, was delayed by 15 years.

A launch date of 2007 for the James Webb Space Telescope was the original agenda, but two years prior a "major redesign"[6] became necessary. In another instance, "a ripped sunshield during a practice deployment"[7] set the project back, followed by a series of significant cost overruns.

<hr>

6 Victoria Bryan, NASA delays launch of Webb telescope after preparation incident – www.aerotime.aero/articles/129522-nasa-delays-launch-of-webb-telescope
7 Victoria Bryan

A picture of the sunshield undergoing tests

In 2012, the House of Representatives voted to eliminate the budget for NASA's Webb project, thereby terminating the program. This nearly spelled the end for the telescope that aimed to "rewrite the textbooks"[8] of the next generation. At that time, the project got out of hand, coming in at $1.6 billion over budget, and it experienced "serious management problems."[9] However, none of the money was wasted, and the technical progress made was of excellent quality. The new telescope had become a "powerful symbol of U.S. leadership in science and space. [Congress] could save a few billion, but to lose it would be wasteful and short-sighted."[10] Fortunately, the budget was soon recovered.

Several new obstacles delayed the launch, but NASA believed that it was finally prepared to proceed in 2020 after completion of construction four years prior. Then came the COVID pandemic, and 2020 became the year of "delayed events,"[11] with the launch of the most sophisticated space telescope in history proving to be no exception.

The increase in excitement was palpable. Scientists had

---

[8] Michael S. Turner, Much More Than a Telescope, *Science*, JSTOR, Reed College

[9] Michael S. Turner

[10] Michael S. Turner

[11] Scot Devlin, Mark Harwood, What You Need to Know About the James Webb Space Telescope, Creation.com, Dec. 26, 2021 – www.creation.com/the-james-webb-space-telescope

viewed much of the universe through Hubble, almost as it was when it was formed, but they learned that none of these galaxies were the first ones formed. Then ultimately realized that "Hubble wasn't the right instrument to detect those first galaxies."[12] "The farther we can see in space, the farther we can see in time…and that's not a metaphor. That's actually literally true,"[13] explained scientist Amber Straughn. The Webb Space Telescope represents "looking in a part of space that we've never seen before."[14] The telescope will be able to detect the earliest galaxies because of its unparalleled sensitivity. Another factor is the kind of light it will collect, "light that our eyes aren't designed to see."[15]

[12] Nasa.gov/ Our Cosmic Time Machine, Host Padi Boyd, Astronomer Amber Straughn, The James Webb Space Telescope, Oct. 6, 2020 – www.nasa.gov/mediacast/our-cosmic-time-machine-the-james-webb-space-telescope

[13] Nasa.gov, Padi Boyd, Amber Straughn

[14] Nasa.gov, Padi Boyd, Amber Straughn

[15] Nasa.gov, Padi Boyd, Amber Straughn

The First Telescopes

The magnification of objects, microscopic and at great distances, has inspired an inquiry of Earth's environment, involving creation itself. In the fields of astronomy and cosmology, four brief centuries have taken astronomers from small glass mirrors built by eyeglass craftsmen to sky-based telescopes, "liberated"[16] from the atmospheric distortion and background light of Earth.

Many milestones originated in 17th century Europe, a time of budding scientific frenzy, and the population at that time must have been awestruck by the introduction of lenses. Space devotees in the 20th and 21st centuries must be no less stimulated by the unthinkably powerful telescopes operating today in a low orbit around Earth. Early telescopes opened up space to the human race, whereas today's instruments can look back into time.

In 1608, a Dutch eyeglass maker, Hans Lippershey, patented a comparatively primitive telescope under the simple name of "*Kijker*," or "looker."[17] Some claim Lippershey stole the design from fellow eyeglass merchant Jacob Metius, who applied for a patent a few weeks later. Both were rejected due to a number of counterclaims and an official opinion that such a device was easily copied. Jansen went on to design the first

[16] McFadden, 2020

[17] McFadden, 2020

compound telescope, and both he and Lippershey received awards for their work.

HANS LIPPERHEY.
secundus Conspiciliorum inventor.

An engraving of Lippershey

The Lippershey design came to the attention of Jacques Bovedere of Paris. He reported it to Galileo Galilei of Florence, who built his own telescope, and it is Galileo who has garnered the lion's share of credit for the telescope's concept. To be fair, the Galileo model increased the magnification of previous efforts by 20 times. With this instrument, he was able to draw the

Moon's phases in detail, he discovered the rings around Saturn, and he could see four of Jupiter's moons. Galileo's design was powerful enough to detect a diffuse ribbon of light in the night sky, later identified as the Milky Way. Through his observations, Galileo was convinced that Copernicus's heliocentric model was correct, an opinion that caused him to be held under house arrest until the year of his death.

Galileo

Johannes Kepler contributed to the early 17th century with the Keplerian telescope. A German mathematician and astronomer, Kepler was an astrologer as well, before those fields parted ways in the modern age. Considered "the father of modern optics,"[18] he designed an instrument of two convex lenses, increasing the magnification but delivering the image to the viewer upside down.

Christian Huygens, a Dutch scientist, mathematician, and founder of the wave theory of light, used his own system to find another moon in 1655. The instrument was devoted to the study of the planets and solar system. Huygens introduced ocular and aerial (tubeless) telescopes and made early use of the micrometer. Assembling a 12-foot instrument, he confirmed "Saturni Luna," or Titan.

Sir Isaac Newton built the first reflecting telescope (as opposed to "refracting") in 1668. In his simple system called the "Newton reflector," a concave primary mirror was set against a flat, diagonal second pane. The piece has become the earliest known functioning reflecting telescope. In his work with the light spectrum, Newton used what some have described as a crude spectrometer. However, the modern instrument was invented a century later by Gustav Kirchhoff and Robert Benson, and its ability to split light into constituent wavelengths became

---

[18] McFadden, 2020

an invaluable part of space exploration technology.

Newton

Laurent Cassegrain employed another simple design near the end of the 17th century, called the "Cassegrain reflector," based on a folded double-mirror. Cassegrain was a Catholic priest with an ongoing interest in science and astronomy, teaching science classes in his late career.

One of the first large telescopes, measuring 40 feet in length, was built in 1789 by William Herschel in Britain. The largest in the late 19th century was built in Wisconsin as the centerpiece of the Yerkes Observatory.

The concept of a space telescope was theorized in 1923 by German rocket scientist Herman Oberth, who suggested such a "space-bound" instrument in his book, *Die Rakete zu den Planeträumen.* In the 1930s, Karl Guthe Jansky set about solving the static problems in the telephone system as an engineer for Bell Telephone Laboratories and discovered radio waves from the Milky Way.

Sir Bernard Lovell conceived of an immense 250-foot disc radio telescope that could be aimed at any point in the sky. American Lyman Spitzer proposed it in 1946, and he lobbied for 30 years to manifest such an instrument. A researcher and professor at Yale University, he continued to argue the advantages of a space-based unit over ground-based examples. At Princeton, Spitzer headed the National Academy of Science Ad Hoc Committee and published the first paper based on a proposed project in the same year.

Spitzer

Lowell

The Concept of a Space Telescope

By the time Lovell was working on his creation, the idea that a telescope in orbit would work much better than on Earth was being explored. In the 1940s, astronomers and scientists speculated that Earth's atmosphere distorted the ability of telescopes to take high resolution images, a distortion referred to as "seeing." This distortion is observable by anyone who stands outside at night and sees stars twinkling. In addition, Earth's atmosphere mostly protects the surface from infrared light and ultraviolet rays, which is good for life but detrimental for astronomy. Finally, all of the light caused by cities and life also affects astronomy done on the surface.

By the mid-20th century, technology had allowed people to create radios and other devices that could detect waves along the entire electromagnetic spectrum. Instead of just seeing light waves, telescopes were designed that could also pick up radio waves, measure radiation and thermal generation with infrared, and even detect x-rays and gamma-rays.

It was Lovell's dream that first broke through with a completed telescope in 1957, but 30 years of theorizing had not yet produced a delivery system for an orbiting instrument. The best Lovell could get was one of the most powerful land-based telescopes, situated in central England, but given that a telescope with all of these abilities would operate better in space, it was just a matter of making such a telescope and getting it into orbit. As rocket technology developed, the Soviet Union and United States were both able to launch satellites into orbit.

The year 1957 was an auspicious one, as the Soviet Union launched Sputnik, the first orbiting satellite. Little more than a 193-pound ball with a beeping mechanism, Sputnik ignited the fiercest phase of the Space Race between the Cold War superpowers. The United States launched its first satellite into orbit only three months later, and NASA was established on October 1, 1958.

The first meeting of Spitzer's committee was held in 1966 as a study of the telescope's possible uses. In 1969, the panel published *Scientific Uses of the Large Space Telescope,* urging that the design and construction of a prototype begin. For this to occur, support from NASA was obligatory. Wernher von Braun, the former Nazi official who became NASA's foremost rocket scientist, had considered the possibilities and recommended a small mirror of 120 inches.

In 1971, George Lowe, then acting administrator at NASA, gave approval to the Large Space Telescope Steering Committee for a series of feasibility studies. At that point, the process of fundraising could begin. Unfortunately, the price was a hefty one at $400 million, a tough sell for a country recovering from World War II and Korea while waging a "police action" in Vietnam. The recent Apollo missions to the Moon had been inspiring, but the costs were not. The request for funding was denied by the House Sub-Committee in 1975, but the ensuing partnership with the European Space Agency proved a diplomatic boon, lowering the overall cost. Following a mirror reduction from the original three meters to 2.4, the financial burden was halved, and the amount of $200 million was passed by Congress in 1977.

The initial progress on Hubble's construction was quick. A contract was awarded to Perkin-Elmer to construct the mirror and optical assembly, and grinding of the primary mirror began in December 1978 in Danbury, Connecticut. Lockheed Missiles and Space Company, located in Sunnyvale, California, was engaged to build the spacecraft and all support systems. By the next year, future maintenance issues once the telescope was in orbit were anticipated, and training missions began for repairs, replacements, and updates for all components.

Computer-based lens-grinding provided a mirror so fine that a world-sized version would have no flaw above six inches, but when an optimistic launch date of 1983 was announced, it was subsequently interrupted by several factors. The first was an incomplete optical assembly, despite completion of the mirror, so the timeline was pushed further back to 1984. That date was not met, as optical issues took another five years to resolve. Another launch was set for 1986, but on January 28 of that year, the *Challenger* shuttle disaster halted the program for a period of two years.

A picture of the grinding of the mirror

A backup mirror produced by Kodak

The Hubble Space Telescope would not be the only space-based telescope, but the limitations of similar projects were exposed by Hubble's abilities. The telescope was appropriately named for Edwin Hubble, a leading observational cosmologist of the 20th century who all but established the field of observational extragalactic astronomy. Like his namesake telescope, Hubble "changed the way we thought of the universe forever."[19] With a Ph.D. in astronomy at Chicago University, he was invited by George Ellery Hale, founder of the Mount Wilson Observatory in Pasadena, California, to join the staff. The invitation came as Hubble was putting the finishing touches on his thesis and preparing for an oral examination. Hubble's telegram to Hale was surprising: "Regret cannot accept your invitation. Am off to war."[20] He enlisted in the infantry, returned to the U.S. five years later, and eventually found his way to Mount Wilson.

---

[19] "The Man," 2012

[20] "Hubble Overview," 2020

Hubble

Four years after his return, Hubble observed what he believed was a nova star flaring in the Andromeda Nebula. He later realized he had seen a "variable star,"[21] officially known as a "Cepheid" that could be used to measure distance. From that point, he began a study of nebulae, and within a few years, Hubble realized that the universe was expanding at a high rate of speed. This

---

[21] "Hubble Overview," 2020

resulted in what came to be called Hubble's Law. It is, in effect, a statement of "direct correlation between the distance to a galaxy and its recessional velocity as determined by the red shift."[22] Hubble assisted in the design and construction of the Hale 200-inch telescope on Palomar Mountain, and he was the first individual to use the instrument.

The European Space Agency contributed important technology to the long-struggling project, including the Faint Object Camera, the first two solar wings that power the craft, and an excellent team of scientists and engineers at the Space Telescope Science Institute in Baltimore, Maryland. Since Hubble's launch, Europe has been given 15% of the telescope's observation time. The Hubble Project's European Science Archive is located at the European Space Astronomy Centre [sic] (ESAC) near the city of Madrid. Up to 2012, it was hosted by the Space Telescope European Coordinating Facility of the European Southern Observatory near Munich. The Space Telescope Science Institute selects the telescope's targets and processes the data from the Johns Hopkins University's Homewood Campus in Baltimore. All control of the aircraft is handled at the Goddard Space Flight Center in Maryland.

---

[22] Nave, 2005

The case for a space-based observatory is by now clear to anyone involved in the ground-based telescope industry or any student of astronomy. Light traversing the known universe, seen billions of years into its journey, is distorted, interacting with Earth's atmosphere, like viewing an object through a vessel of water. Such distortions can be seen in the "twinkling" of the stars. Not only does a space telescope eliminate distortions, but in Hubble's case, the viewing spectrum from infrared through visible and ultraviolet wavelengths is available.

A picture of construction on the Hubble telescope

The Hubble telescope laid the groundwork for future deep space exploration and set the template for how to operate a space telescope. Newton once famously wrote, "If I have seen further, it is by standing on the shoulders of giants." After the publication of 15,000 academic papers based on the Hubble Space Telescope's investigations and its collection of superb photos, present and future missions will continue to rely on that telescope's decades of data-gathering as primary sources.

Advanced Components

To get a telescope such as Webb prepared for launch, it must go through a relentless barrage of testing. A year before liftoff, the unit was put on a vibration table and subjected to a "simulated launch."[23] The entire unit was vibrated at a rate of 100 times per second, and as the launch date drew near, scientists reminisced back to the earliest days of the project. At that time, the committee incessantly sent back the same message: "Bigger and colder."[24]

On December 18, 2021, the launch was again delayed following an "incident"[25] during final preparations. The sudden "unplanned release of a clamp band securing Webb to the launch vehicle adapter caused a vibration throughout the observatory."[26] "The most delayed

---

[23] Nasa.gov, Padi Boyd, Amber Straughn

[24] Nasa.gov, Padi Boyd, Amber Straughn

[25] Victoria Bryan

[26] Victoria Bryan

telescope in history"[27] was finally launched on December 25, 2021.

[27] Big Think, Ten Unbelievable but True Facts about NASA's James Webb Space Telescope – www.bigthink.com/starts-with-a-bang/10-facts-james-webb

Pictures of the telescope on the launchpad

A picture of the payload with the telescope in space

Webb was billed as the "First Light Machine"[28] due to its ability to observe the earliest known light at such great distances. A vastly larger instrument than Hubble, the Webb telescope is not merely a super-sized duplicate of its predecessor but works primarily in the infrared range of the light spectrum, with some optical capacity. Hubble was the opposite as primarily an optical telescope.

Following its successful launch, Webb was positioned far from the reaches of Earth's ability to repair it, approximately a million miles away. At such a distance, there is no room for mistakes. Provided all goes well, it will peer much farther back in time than was possible with Hubble to capture photos of the first generation of

---

[28] Andrew May, James Webb Space Telescope: Origins, Design, and Mission Objectives, March, 2022, Live Science – www.livescience.com/james-webb-space-telescope

galaxies as they existed just following the Big Bang.

NASA's complex creation of this precision instrument represented its "ambitious first scientific endeavor"[29] to answer the most basic and persistent questions about how the universe works. Webb will serve as the "premier observatory for at least the next decade," providing pictures for thousands of astronomers on the ground.

The project was named for James E. Webb, the legendary NASA administrator who crafted the Apollo program and a "staunch supporter of space science."[30] Webb served as the second administrator of NASA. Born on October 7, 1906, in North Carolina, he was educated at the University of North Carolina Chapel Hill. After graduation, he joined the Marines as a pilot before studying law at Georgetown University. Later a secretary to a congressman, he took a job as Assistant to the Undersecretary of the Treasury. In time, Webb became Director of the Bureau of the Budget in the Executive Office of the President, then went on to serve as Undersecretary of State.

After the famous goal of landing on the Moon was announced by President Kennedy, Webb "politicked, coaxed, cajoled, and maneuvered for NASA… [as] a master of bureaucratic politics."[31] He was the leader of

[29] Webb Space Telescope, James Webb Telescope Overview, University of Arizona – www.jwst.arizona.edu/mission/
[30] Scientific Visualization Studio, NASA, James Webb Space Telescope – www.gsfc.gov/Gallery/

NASA when tragedy struck the Apollo 1 mission when three astronauts were killed on the launchpad in a flashfire. Webb took a great deal of abuse for the accident from the government, and he retired as Apollo was completing its most successful missions.

Webb

---

[31] James E. Webb, NASA Administrator, Feb. 14, 1961 – Oct. 7, 1968 – www.history.nasa.gov/biographies/webb.html

While he remains most renowned for the historic successes of the Apollo program, there has been pressure from some quarters to rename the telescope due to Webb's alleged hiring abuses of LGBTQ scientists. When the decision to name the telescope after Webb was made in the early 21st century, little was known of Webb's role in the so-called "Lavender Scare,"[32] a witch hunt during which many gay and lesbian federal employees were seen as security risks and subsequently surveilled and fired. Among some of the team members, there was "[s]adness, disappointment, frustration and anger"[33] at the choice. Some of the reactions of astronomers over NASA's decision to rename the telescope have gone overtly public, once newly revealed evidence suggested that Webb was involved in "persecution of gay and lesbian federal employees during the 50s and 60s."[34] Over 400 pages were released in a Freedom of Information request. Yao-Yuan Mao of Rutgers University laments that LGBTQ concerns among the scientific community "are not really what they care about."[35] Bernard Scott Gaudi, an astronomer at Ohio State University, remarked, "It's almost amusing how incompetent the whole thing was."[36]

The James Webb Space Telescope was created in a

---

[32] Scientific American

[33] Scientific American, New Revelations, Pressure on NASA to Rename the James Webb Space Telescope – www.scientificamerican.com/article/new-news-raise-pressure-on-nasa-to-rename-the-james-webb-space-telescope/

[34] Scientific American

[35] Scientific American

[36] Scientific American

partnership between NASA, the European Space Agency (EAS), and the Canadian Space Agency (CSA). NASA oversees the Webb program and takes responsibility for funding the project, but the various systems, components, and processes were widely distributed between a variety of partners, each with specific skills.

The Goddard Space Flight Center provided the ISIM (Integrated Science Instrument Module) components, the Jet Propulsion Laboratory manages the Mid-Infrared Instrument, and the Ames Research Center serves as the directing body of Technology Development. The Johnson Space Center provides observatory test facilities, and the Marshall Space Flight Center took the lead in Mirror Technology, Development and Environmental Research. The Glenn Research Center is in charge of the Cryogenic Component Development. Academic and industrial partners include Ball Aerospace, the Harris Corporation, Lockheed Martin, Northrop Grumman, the Space Telescope Science Institute, and the University of Arizona. NASA awarded the Ground Systems and Systems of Engineering contract to KBR Wyle Services of Greenbelt, Maryland. The contract includes all facility engineering, launch and early orbit support, flight operations, flight dynamics support, and sustained engineering for NASA. Infrared cameras were provided by the University of Arizona, and the Near-Infrared

Spectrograph was created by the European Space Agency. Its components were provided by NASA and the Goddard Space Flight Center. The Mid-Infrared Instrument (MIRI) came from the European Consortium from the ESA and the Jet Propulsion Laboratory. The Fine Guidance Sensor (the Near-Infrared Imager and the Slitless Spectrograph (FGS/NIRISS) were created by the Canadian Space Agency (CSA).

Ball Aerospace designed and built the advanced optical technology and lightweight mirror system. Ball also designed the Webb mirror's control electronics to operate in a "deep freeze cryogenic space environment."[37]

---

[37] Ball.com, Webb Space Telescope – www.ball.com/aerospace/programs/astrophysics/webb

A picture of part of the telescope's mirror in development

A picture of mirror components undergoing cryogenic tests

The Harris Corporation signed an agreement with the Johnson Space Center of NASA to complete "thermal vacuum testing,"[38] validating its ability to operate in space's freezing environment. Harris helped to safeguard the telescope during Hurricane Harvey and tested 1,000 sensors on the telescope around the clock. Harris designed a multi-wavelength interferometer system that aligned the 18 segments into one mirror.

---

[38] Go Photonics, Harris Corporation to Test James Webb Space Telescope for NASA – www.gophotonics.com/details/797/harris-corporation-to-test-james-webb-space-telescope-for-nasa

A picture of the telescope undergoing environmental testing

Engineers at Lockheed Martin designed, assembled, and tested NIRcam, "the primary imager."[39] At the Space Telescope Science Institute of Baltimore, Maryland, engineers "focused for so long on building the telescope,"[40]

[39] Lockheed Martin, James Webb Space Telescope's Powerful Eyes – www.lockheedmartin.com/3n-us/news/features/2021/NIRCam-see-universe-in-new-light.html

[40] News.Yahoo.com, A New Window on the Universe is about to Open Wide: Excitement Building at Baltimore Institute for the James Webb Space Telescope's Observations – www.news.yahoo.com/window-universe-open-wide-excitement-090000710.html

it was a gripping moment to see it complete. Lee Feinberg, Webb's Optical Telescope Manager for 20 years, "The engineers, when we simulated this thing…we simulated a star, never thinking that we'd see galaxies."[41]

A picture of the NIRcam

The University of Arizona led the design and development of the Near-Infrared camera. University professor of Astronomy Regents' Professor Marcia Rieke, the Principal Investigator for NIRCam, led the development of the instrument later built by Lockheed Martin. George Rieke, also a Regens Professor, is the science team's lead for the MIRI (Mid-Infrared

[41] News.Yahoo.com

Instrument) later built by the European Space Consortium.

On February 4, 2021, Dr. Aprille Ericsson of the Webb team received the Ralph Coates Roe Medal from the American Society for Mechanical Engineering. The award honored her international work, "encouraging young people, women and people from other underrepresented groups to pursue STEM careers."[42] This award began to draw attention to the Webb project, first through academia and then the public at large. On February 11, a week later, a media teleconference was held to share progress regarding the early stages of aligning the mirrors. On March 16, a virtual media briefing was held to update the mirror alignment, drawing a surprising degree of interest.

A picture of a model of the telescope on public

[42] Goddard Space Flight Center, James Webb Space Telescope – www.jwst.nasa.gov

Although Hubble and Webb share a certain degree of visible range capability, they are entirely different instruments constructed for different purposes. The James Webb Space Telescope is able to look much farther back than Hubble, whose main mirror is only eight feet in diameter, limiting its ability to observe the most distant objects. Light coming from so far away is stretched due to expansion of the universe, transforming into infrared wave lengths. These are not easy to detect for Hubble, but it is the James Webb Space Telescope's greatest asset.

Despite its superior size to Hubble, the James Webb Space Telescope is "actually lighter,"[43] with a mass of 14,300 pounds to Hubble's 24,500. The James Webb Space Telescope and Hubble do not share the same components or mission, with their dedicated instruments making each "a different type of instrument altogether."[44] Infrared is optimized for a 600 to 2,800 micron capability. Webb cannot see green or blue light, only red and orange, plus a far wider range of longer wavelengths. Webb's mission requires that the instrument be stationed far from Earth to prevent its functions from being blocked by the planet's atmosphere, as Earth produces its own infrared emissions via heat radiation. This tends to "swamp"[45] the

---

[43] Big Think

[44] Andrew May

[45] Andrew May

instrument's ability to detect fainter sources. One side of the sunshield is positioned to face the Sun at all times, so the James Webb Space Telescope requires both heating and cooling. The cool side accomplishes the observations, while the hot side carries all the solar panels and the Earth-oriented antenna.

The location of the telescope's final position from which it will do all its work is known as L2. This is a special location, one of five, where an object can orbit the Sun and always keep the Sun and Earth in the same direction. These locations are known as Lagrangian Points, named for Joseph-Louis Lagrange, who studied them in the 18th century. In these spots, two massive bodies "conspire to keep a third, smaller body in a fixed position."[46] From L2, all bright sources of light emit constant rays from the same direction.

The L2 (Lagrangian Point #2) is rapidly establishing itself as a "preeminent location"[47] for advanced space probes. The ESA has a number of missions that will make use of this "orbital 'sweet spot' in the coming years."[48]

The balancing properties of such locations can be used by spacecraft to "hover"[49] in place. L2 resides four times

[46] Andrew May

[47] Science and Exploration, L2, The Second Lagrangian Point –
    www.esa.int/Science_Exploration/Space_Science/L2_the_second_Lagrangian_Point

[48] Science and Exploration

[49] Science and Exploration

further away from Earth than the Moon ever gets, and it orbits the Sun at the same rate as the Earth. By making constant orbits around the Earth, "passing in and out of [its] shadow and causing it to heat up and cool down"[50] is no longer necessary. It is speculated that at some point in the future, artificial Lagrangian points can be created via a constant force created by solar sails.

NASA has estimated that the polishing error rate of the large primary mirror amounts to less than one millionth of an inch. The power to collect light is in proportion to its aura rather than to its diameter. Thus, it is considerably more powerful than the Hubble. The instrument brings in sunshine at a constant rate, which is healthy for the equipment in the Spacecraft Bus but dangerous for the optical instruments and science module. The power to amass a prodigious amount of light for distant observation has led some to compare Webb to a "time machine,"[51] viewing objects in the form they held nearly 13 billion years ago.

The satellite is stabilized by its Trim Flap. The Solar Power array always faces toward the Sun, and powers the observatories. The antenna pointing toward Earth sends science data back to NASA and in turn receives commands from the Deep Space Network. The Spacecraft

---

[50] Science and Exploration
[51] Andrew May

Bus contains most of the spacecraft steering and control machinery including the computer and reaction wheels.

The Star Tracker is comprised of small tiles that use star patterns to target the observatory. The sunshield is fashioned in five layers to shield the observatory from light and heat of the Sun, and from the Earth. A secondary mirror gathers light from the primary mirror and sends it into the science instruments.

The sunshield is approximately the same size as a full tennis court. Despite the size of the Ariane 5 rocket, both the mirror and sunshade were too large a fit fully open. Both were required to be folded, for a subsequent, command-controlled unfolding in distant space. The temperature between the two sides of the sunshield in which both heating and cooling are required should maintain a difference of 600 degrees Fahrenheit.

The primary mirror is divided into 18 hexagonal segments made of beryllium and is coated with gold to "capture faint infrared light."[52] The gold covering of the mirror contains only "a golf ball's"[53] worth of the mineral, so thin that "a strand of human hair is a thousand times thicker."[54] The reason for such a thin gold covering is due to gold's malleability even at low temperatures. Gold

---

[52] NASA, James Webb Space Telescope – www.nasa.gov/mission_pages/webb/team/index.html
[53] NASA
[54] Sophie Lewis

expands and contracts with small changes which is a "dealbreaker"[55] for mirror technology. However, beryllium "shines on this front."[56] The main mirror is 6.5 meters in diameter, approximately 21.3 feet, all undercast in beryllium which serves to "attenuate heat"[57] from the Sun one million times.

The gold is applied by a process called "vacuum vapor deposition."[58] The mirror segments are placed into an airless chamber into which a small amount of gold vapor is injected. Materials not to be coated are masked off, and the thickness of the gold is set at about nanometers, equivalent to approximately 600 gold molecules. However, the gold is never exposed to space, but is rather coated in a thin layer of amorphous silicon dioxide glass.

At full assembly, the primary mirror makes for the brightest large telescope of all time, weighing 551 pounds. The back side of the mirror is machined away to retain its precise shape, even under the stress of launch. It's designed to resist breaking under vibrations and tension, "despite its brittle nature."[59] A fully exposed mirror is designed to survive an expected number and speed of micro-meteoroid impacts. It is sensitive to needed changes in shape through the use of actuators attached to the back.

---

[55] Big Think

[56] Big Think

[57] James Webb Telescope Overview, University of Arizona

[58] Big Think

[59] Big Think

The inability to repair the Webb Space Telescope means that the correction of the mirror imperfection with custom "spectacles" accomplished with Hubble can never be duplicated. However, the optical systems of the observatory appear to be "working in near flawless fashion."[60] Eventually, the 18 segments of the primary mirror "need to be lined up to within a few nanometers (billionth of a meter) of one another."[61] In a trial run of the Near-Infrared NIRCam, identifying dots of starlight from the same star in each panel of the mirror captured 1,560 images over a 25-hour period, "a giant mosaic with more than two billion pixels."[62] The telescope sits comfortably at L2, which has the additional meaning in shorthand for Second Language Point where gravity from the Sun and the Earth balance the orbital motion of a satellite.

While the instrument is working on the fourth stage of mirror alignment through March of 2022, a process called "Coarse Phasing,"[63] other projects move forward. One is to measure and correct small height differences between mirror segments. At the same time, Webb's Near-Infrared Spectrograph has successfully completed a "check-out

---

[60] William Harwood, CBS News, NASA's Webb Telescope Achieves Near-Perfect Focus, March 16, 2022 – www.cbsnews.com/news/nasa-webb-telescope-near-perfect-focus

[61] William Harwood

[62] Ashley Strickland, CNN, Webb Telescope's First Test Images Include an Unexpected 'Selfie' - www.cnn.com/2022.02/11/wortld/james-webb-space-telescope-selfie-images-scn/index.htsh

[63] Blogs.nasa.gov, Checking Out Mechanisms in Webb's NIRSpec Instrument – www.blogs.nasa.gov/webb/2022/03/03/checking-out-the-mechanisms-in-webbs-nirspec-instrument

and initial characterization of three crucial mechanisms"[64] contained within. The inner workings include a Filter Wheel Assembly (FWA), a Grating Wheel Assembly (GWA), and a Refocus Mechanism Assembly (RMA).

The gratings in the GWA "spread incoming light over its colors or wavelengths"[65] to make a spectrum. Filters in the FWA block the wavelengths "outside the range of interest"[66] to prevent contamination between optical paths, or "orders."[67] The RMA adjusts the instrument focus. Scientists "operated the Filter Wheel first, cycling it through all eight of its positions in both forward and reverse directions."[68] Data was recorded at each position demonstrating how the wheel was moving.

A similar procedure was followed for the Grating Wheel, which "performed excellently the first time."[69] The Refocus Mechanism Assembly includes a "linear translation stage that holds two mirrors."[70] These are used to fine-tune the instrument focus. Scientists are optimistic that the NIRSpec should be prepared to begin science observations by this summer.

The four instruments are comprised of various cameras,

---

[64] Blogs.nasa.gov

[65] Blogs.nasa.gov

[66] Blogs.nasa.gov

[67] Blogs.nasa.gov

[68] Blogs.nasa.gov

[69] Blogs.nasa.gov

[70] Blogs.nasa.gov

spectrometers that have detectors to reach extremely faint signals. The NIRSpec is outfitted with micro-shutters to enable observation of up to 100 objects at the same time.

The detectors are particularly essential to light gathering and filtering. The mirrors collect light and send it to the instruments. They filter it before focusing it onto the detectors, where photons are "absorbed and ultimately converted into the electronic voltages that we measure."[71] The instrument requires ultra-sensitive detectors to "record the feeble light from far-away galaxies, stars, and planets."[72] A large array of detectors is also needed to more efficiently "survey the sky."[73]

The telescope employs two different types of detectors. The first is managed by a mercury-cadmium-telluride (H2RG) mix for use in the Near-Infrared instruments. The second is governed by arsenic doped silicon for use in the Near-Infrared. In the first example, by varying the ratio of mercury to cadmium, one can tune the material to "sense longer or shorter wavelength light."[74] The ability to tailor each NIRCam detector allows for peak performance.

The process involves an "incident photon"[75] which is absorbed by the semi-conductor, yielding "molecule

---

[71] Goddard Flight Center, James Webb Space Telescope, Infrared Detectors –
www.jwst.nasa.gov/content/about/innovations/infrared.html
[72] Goddard Flight Center, Infrared Detectors
[73] Goddard Flight Center, Infrared Detectors
[74] Goddard Flight Center, Infrared Detectors
[75] Goddard Flight Center, Infrared Detectors

election hole pairs."[76] These move under the influence of "built-in and applied electronic fields"[77] "until they find their way"[78] to a collection point.

NASA's Spitzer Telescope, a sister instrument of Hubble, was forced to switch over to a "warm mission"[79] once it had run out of coolant. Webb, on the other hand, should maintain cold temperatures for its entire life span. When it does run out of fuel, it will "permanently reside in a 'graveyard orbit' around the Sun."[80]

The Webb is required to expend fuel whenever it needs to move at all, either to correct a course, perform orbital corrections to stay at L2, or to orient itself to a desired target. Speculation among scientists holds that the general instrument could someday be robotically refueled, so a refueling port has been included when and if we can figure out how to get there. Most likely, by that time, a successor telescope will have been built.

The NIRCam, NIRSpec, the Fine Guidance System and the Near-Infrared Imager and Spectrograph (FGS/NIRISS) will inevitably reach their temperature target range from 34 to 39 kelvins through passive cooling. From that point, it must be cooled down to seven

---

[76] Goddard Flight Center, Infrared Detectors

[77] Goddard Flight Center, Infrared Detectors

[78] Goddard Flight Center, Infrared Detectors

[79] Big Think

[80] Big Think

kelvins or less, which is not possible on Webb by passive means alone. The Cryocooler employs Helium gas to carry heat from MIRI's optics and detectors out to the warm side of the sunshield and provides heat to "protect sensitive components from the risk of ice forming."[81] This process provides a progressive adjustment to ensure a "slow, controlled stable cooldown for the instrument."[82] Soon, the team will bring the MIRI instrument temperature down to minus 447 degrees Fahrenheit, minus 266 Celsius, in order for it to function.

To "integrate all instrument systems and sub-systems is a daunting endeavor"[83] due to their various needs and temperature requirements. Engineers divided ISIM into three primary regions. "Region1"[84] holds the main component for the Cryogenics Instrument Module and the OTE Thermal Management Subsystem to provide passing cooling.

"Region 2"[85] holds the bulk of the Electronics Compartment, providing the "mounting surfaces and ambient thermally controlled environment for the instrument control electronics."[86] "Region 3"[87] handles the component of the ISIM Command and Data Handling

---

[81] Goddard Space Flight Center, James Webb Space Telescope – www.jwst.nasa.gov
[82] Goddard Space Flight Center
[83] NASA
[84] NASA
[85] NASA
[86] NASA
[87] NASA

Subsystem located in the Spacecraft Bus with integral ISIM flight software, the MIRI Cryocooler Compressor and Control Electronics.

At present, the Webb Space Telescope is just "chilling out…literally…after several months of nail-biting sky maneuvers and some stunning initial images."[88] At higher temperatures, any signal that may be detected from the sky "is lost beneath the signal from its own internally generated 'dark current,'"[89] explains Alistair Glasse, a Webb MIRI instrument scientist at the Astronomy Technology Centre in the UK, and Macarena Garcia-Marin of the EAS.

That is the answer to the question, "Why develop an instrument with such a fussy temperature range?"[90] It all has to do with the range of light in which it can see. "Mid-Infrared light can pass through 20 times thicker clouds than visible light,"[91] says Klaus Pontopiddan at the Space Telescope Science Institute. Young stars form quickly in under 100,000 years. "Their natal clouds have not yet had time to disperse, hiding what is going on in this critical stage from visible view."[92]

The essential cryocooler is on board for cooling the mid-

---

[88] Cosmos Magazine Newsletter, What's the James Webb Space Telescope Up to Now? – www.cosmosmagazine.com/space/astronomy/james-webb-space-telescope-cooling

[89] Cosmos Magazine

[90] Cosmos Magazine

[91] Cosmos Magazine

[92] Cosmos Magazine

infrared detectors of another instrument, the Mid-Infrared Instrument (MIRI). The telescope passively cools itself to no higher than 50 kelvins, cool enough to make nitrogen liquefy. This is part of the reason why it must be situated far from Earth's orbit, as the heat emitted from Earth would prevent the instrument from reaching the required low temperatures.

   The cryocooler is operating "cryogenic valves"[93] that will redirect Helium gas and force it through a "flow restriction."[94] As the gas expands, exiting the restriction, it becomes colder. It alone can bring the instrument under 7 kelvins. However, first it must make it through the "pinch point"[95] at 15 kelvins where the cryocooler's ability to remove heat is at the lowest point. The process will require "several carefully timed switches in the valves and compressor,"[96] sensitively balanced so that MIRI neither cools too much nor begins to warm."[97] MIRI will be "the last of the four instruments to open its eyes to the universe."[98] During its "chilling" period, James Webb Space Telescope has safely arrived to its "operation orbit"[99] approximately 1.5 million kilometers from Earth, squarely in the L2 position.

---

[93] Cosmos Magazine

[94] Cosmos Magazine

[95] Cosmos Magazine

[96] Cosmos Magazine

[97] Cosmos Magazine

[98] Cosmos Magazine

[99] Webb Space Telescope, University of Arizona

Serving all "internal refrigeration"[100] to establish and maintain the right cryogenic temperature for the MIRI, the cryocooler's specific function is to keep detectors cold. Northrup Grumman has delivered to date more than 50 flight cryocoolers with an accumulated 300 years of combined on-orbit operations.

Webb at Work

The telescope is designed to collect infrared radiation through its 21-foot primary mirror. The telescope can observe hidden and fainter objects in this manner. However, it must look at one patch of the universe for a considerably longer time to collect as much light as possible for the distance of the objects astronomers seek to view.

Unlike visual telescopes, this one can peer through the dust of planetary and star birth chambers. Among its first assignments will be to observe and analyze the newly-formed star Beta Pictoris, part of a gamut of observations scheduled through the first year. Before the James Webb Space Telescope was fully conceived, "multiple new technologies had to be invented just to build it."[101] Mission objectives were added along the way as their possibility became known.

---

[100] Innotech Today, An Inside Look at Cryocooler Tech for the James Webb Telescope – www.innotechtoday.com/an-inside-llok-at-cryocooler-tech-fir-the-james-webb-telescope

[101] Northrop Grumman, James Webb Space Telescope – www.northropgrumman.com/space/james-webb-space-telescope/

The detection of infrared heat easily pierces dust clouds within these "star birth" chambers. In the birth of new planetary systems, Webb can study organic molecules important for life to develop. A century ago, astronomers did not know that stars are driven by nuclear fusion, and even 50 years ago, they did not yet recognize that stars are continually forming. Now, astronomers are hoping to soon see the details of "how clouds of gas and dust collapse to form stars, or why stars form mostly in groups, or exactly how planetary systems form."[102]

With the Webb telescope, the study of star and planet formation may "allow us to connect observations of mature exoplanets to their birth environments and our own solar system to its own origins."[103] Both young stars and giant planets "begin their lives as large, puffy structures that contract over time."[104] Young stars become hotter as they mature while giant planets cool, and "both typically emit more light in the infrared than at visible wavelengths."[105]

The infrared range, also called the "molecular fingerprint region,"[106] is ideal for identifying the presence of a range of chemicals, in particular "water and various organics."[107]

---

[102] Blogs.NASA, James Webb Space Telescope, Webb's Cool View on How Stars, Planets Form – www.blogs.nasa.gov/webb/2022/04/07/webbs-cool-view-on-how-stars-and-planets-form/

[103] Blogs.NASA

[104] Blogs.NASA

[105] Blogs.NASA

[106] Blogs.NASA

[107] Blogs.NASA

All four of Webb's instruments can detect various important molecules using their "spectroscopic modes."[108] They are "particularly sensitive to molecular ices present in cold molecular clouds before stars are formed."[109]

The NIRSpec will "comprehensively map the spatial distribution of ices"[110] to help scientists understand the underlying chemistry. MIRI will observe warm molecular gases near many young stars where "rocky, potentially habitable planets may be forming."[111]

[108] Blogs.NASA

[109] Blogs.NASA

[110] Blogs.NASA

[111] Blogs.NASA

A component of the NIRspec instrument

Within the clouds that defy visible wavelengths, the reddish colors indicate thicker dust with temperatures less than minus 400 degrees Fahrenheit. Clouds that created protostars collapse into a disc of immense proportions and "continue to accumulate gas and dust for thousands of years."[112]

---

[112] Britannica.com, Envision the birth of stars and planets illuminated through the infrared eye of the James Webb Space Telescope – www.britannica.com/video/154216/James-Webb-Space-Telescope-stars

One feature of large galaxies is the presence of "supermassive black holes"[113] in their centers. These power quasars, bright galactic nuclei. Webb is expected to study six of the most "distant and luminous"[114] examples of these phenomena. Vivienne Baldassare, Assistant Professor of Physics and Astronomy at Washington State University, is part of a research team that plans to use Webb for the study of black holes. Baldassare intends to determine whether star clusters and small galaxies have black holes in their centers.

The question does not stop with their presence, but in gauging their weight to help explain their formation. All massive galaxies have supermassive black holes, most with a mass "billions of times that of the Sun,"[115] and the Webb telescope will enable Baldassare and her team of collaborators to search for telltale signs 65 million light years away in the Virgo Cluster. They will search for gravitational distortions caused by black holes on the stars, gas, and space surrounding them. Smaller black holes may only carry a mass of 100,000 times that of the Sun, which makes their analysis more difficult.

Baldassare's team, led by Matthew Taylor of Canada's Herzberg Institute of Astrophysics, hopes to collect data

---

[113] Andrew May

[114] Andrew May

[115] William Ferguson, WSU Insider, WSU Physicist to Study Black Holes with the James Webb Telescope, Dec. 7, 2021 – www.wsu.edu/press-release/2021/12/07

within the coming year. Other fascinations for the team include the "glow" from the first stars to shine in the universe, which Webb is fine-tuned to locate. A primary goal is to detect and study "some of the earliest black holes that formed in the early universe."[116]

Nico Cappelluti will compete for observation time with Baldassare and countless others with his black hole research. As Professor of Astrophysics at the University of Miami, he noted, "Infrared light is the signature of distant objects, and that's what the James Webb will allow us to see."[117] Cappelluti added, "We have no idea why supermassive black holes are so big, because they didn't have time to grow to such enormous sizes. We're trying to see if they account for the missing matter in the universe, which is dark matter."[118]

Cappelluti and others will employ other instruments in conjunction with Webb: "Astrophysical objects emit light at every wavelength, from X-ray to radio."[119] The Chandra X-Ray Observatory and LISA (Laser Interferometer Space Antenna, set for a 2037 launch) will eventually be added to Webb's data.

The rush is on to study the supermassive black hole at

---

[116] William Ferguson

[117] UNews@the U, Nasa's Webb Telescope will help unlock secrets of black holes – www.nasa.miam.edu/stories/2022/01/nasa-webb-telescope-will-help-unlock-secrets-of-black-holes.html

[118] UNews@ the U

[119] UNews @ the U

the center of the Milky Way, as soon as the "Scheduling Sudoku"[120] is set. The Milky Way's black hole is known as Sagittarius A. The aim is to study, among other aspects, mysterious "unique flickering flares"[121] in the material surrounding it. It is the only known black hole to exhibit this feature.

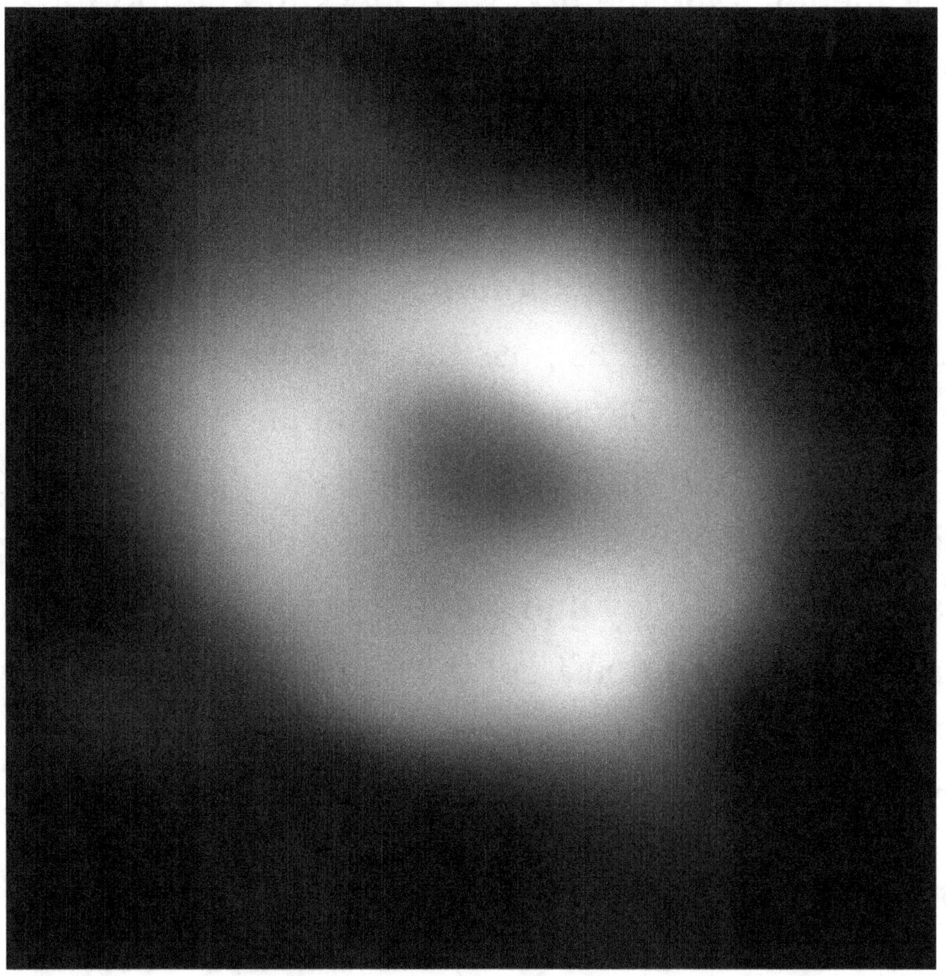

A recent picture taken of the Milky Way's supermassive black hole

[120] NASA.gov, Goddard, NASA's Webb will Join Forces with the Event Horizon Telescope to Reveal the Milky Way's Supermassive Black Hole – www.nasa.gov/feature/goddard/2021/nasa-s-webb-will-join-forces-with-the-event-horizon-telescope-to-reveal-the-milky-way-supermassive-black-hole

[121] NASA.gov, Goddard

Acquiring enough observation time is difficult, but astronomers agree that the effort is worth it. "It's the noblest thing humans can do,"[122] said Farhad Yusef-Zadeh of Northwestern University. Misty Bentz of Georgia State University cited an investigation into the black hole at the center of the Spiral Galaxy, using Webb to weigh the phenomenon. One method is to measure the motion of the stars under a black hole's pull of gravity. She observed, "The heavier the black hole, the faster nearby stars will move under its gravitational influence."[123]

The aim of the observation mission is to reach objects as near to the Big Bang as possible. Marusa Bradac, astronomer at UC Davis, is quoted in an NPR interview as saying, "We are trying to build up a story of how the first galaxies ever emerged and how these evolved with galaxies we see today and we live in today."[124] Bradac continued, "If you don't get the beginning right, it's really difficult to figure out what the whole evolution looked like."[125]

The first six months from launch to fully operational science studies were carefully scheduled. Webb was carried aloft on an Ariane 5 rocket and the launch took

---

[122] NASA.gov, Goddard

[123] Christine Pulliam, Space Telescope Institute, Baltimore, MD, How to Weight a Black Hole Using NASA's Webb Space Telescope – www.nasa.gov/feature/goddard/2018/how-to-weigh-a-black-hole-using-nasa-s-webb-space-telescope

[124] Chris Holt, How the James Webb Telescope Will Peer Back in Time, April 5, 2022, Discover – www.discovermagazine.com/the-sciences/how-the-james-webb-space-telescope-will-peer-back-in-time

[125] Chris Holt

place at the Guiana Space Centre in Kouru, French Guiana. The Ariane 5 provided thrust for the telescope for a period of 26 minutes and telemetry began after the payload fairing separation three and a half minutes after launch. Webb separated from the Ariane 5 one half hour following ignition and the Solar Ray deployed automatically immediately following. After that, several systems were released that had been locked during launch on command. Two hours following launch, the high antenna was deployed. Approximately 12 hours later, the first trajectory correction maneuver was accomplished by small rocket engines aboard the telescope itself. The second trajectory correction maneuver was made about 60 hours after liftoff. Only after these maneuvers were complete did the sequence of major deployments begin.

The first large items to deploy were the fore and aft sunshield pallets, followed by release of the remaining sub-system launch locks. Once the shields were deployed in an uncalibrated state, the telescope and the Spacecraft Bus moved apart by about two meters. At this point, the deployable tower assembly was extended. The full sunshield deployment came directly after, with the unfolding and tensioning of the membranes initiated. At six days after launch, the secondary mirror and the side wings of the primary mirror were unfolded. At the end of the month, a mid-course correction was made that ensured achieving Webb's final orbit around L2.

The telescope proceeded to cool near its operating temperature, but the ISIM was warmed with electric heaters to prevent condensation from forming on the instruments. Residual water that had become trapped in the unit escaped into the vacuum of space. As the telescope cooled down in the shade of the sunshield, the warm electronics were turned on and the flight software was initialized by the end of the first month.

By the second month, at 33 days following launch, the Fine Guidance Sensor was turned on for operation, followed by the NIRCam (Near Infrared Camera) and the NIRSpec (Near-Infrared Spectrograph). The first NIRCam image produced by Webb was that of a crowded star field to make sure that sufficient light was passing through the telescope and into the instruments.

The mirror's many segments were not yet fully aligned, so it was assumed that the picture would be out of focus. Scientists were pleasantly surprised by its clarity. 44 days after launch, Webb began the process of adjusting the primary mirror segments, first identifying each mirror segment with its image of a star in the camera. Following that, the secondary mirror was focused.

In the third month following launch, 60 to 90 days out, the primary mirror segments were aligned so that they could work together as a single optical surface. At that time, the MIRI (Mid-Infrared Instrument) began operation. By the end of the third month, Webb was able to produce its first science-quality image. By this time, the instrument had completed its journey to the L2 orbit position.

A picture of the MIRI

Around 85 days out from launch, Webb will have completed the "optimization"[126] of the telescopic image in the NIRCam. For the following month and a half, it will optimize that image for the other instruments. It will then test and calibrate all instrument capabilities by observing representative science targets in the fourth through the

[126] Webb Space Telescope, University of Arizona

sixth month. At the end of six months, the science mission will begin conducting "routine operations."[127] On January 20, scientists and engineers operating the telescope answered questions about the latest milestones in a NASA science live broadcast, followed by a media teleconference.

The mission objectives for the Webb Telescope are quite varied. Among primary pursuits will be to find the first galaxies of the early universe that connect the Big Bang to the Milky Way. Its infrared detection capacity will cut through the dusty clouds surrounding star chambers to witness the creation of planetary systems. Webb will look "right into stellar nurseries."[128] Thus far, all the necessary optics are working successfully, and the expectation is high that the instruments will meet or exceed the goals they were built to achieve.

Beyond viewing the birth of planetary systems, a further goal is to understand "formation of the elements"[129] found there. Scientists are aware that in environments of high temperatures and density, the simplest elements are formed. These include mostly helium and hydrogen, while other elements such as carbon, gold, and silicon are created in nuclear reactions within stars, and in huge stellar explosions called supernovae. These violent events

---

[127] Webb Space Telescope, University of Arizona
[128] Chris Holt
[129] Chris Holt

scattered the elements into the galaxy, but scientists still "don't entirely understand the processes involved."[130]

Designed to observe "celestial objects"[131] more than 13 billion miles away, Webb will devote much of its time to the study of exoplanets. Scientists all over the world can apply for time using the telescope to support their research, and a large percentage of that effort will be spent on exoplanets. The telescope can study the atmospheric makeup of these bodies to detect signs of current or past life, and thousands of new planets have already been discovered in past decades.

The project's goals can be grouped into four themes as the telescope studies "every phase"[132] in the history of the universe, from "the first luminous glows after the Big Bang onward."[133] The first has been referred to as the "End of the Dark Ages: From First Light and Reionization." Second is the assembly of galaxies themselves, comparing the faintest early formations to today's grand spirals and ellipticals in an effort to trace their evolution. The third category involves the birth of stars and protoplanetary systems, while the fourth ties that search into the origins of life itself.

[130] Chris Holt

[131] Paige Sutherland, Tom Skoog, Meghna Chakrabarti, The Remarkable Story of the James Webb Space Telescope – www.wburorg./2022/04/01/nasa-space-story-of-the-webb-space-telescope

[132] Webb Space Telescope, University of Arizona

[133] Webb Space Telescope, University of Arizona

The first targets to be addressed remain top secret although general information is available. It is known that the telescope will study small galaxies, and that the first photos will be released in the summer of 2022. It is also clear that the first targets have been finalized. NASA received more than 1,000 proposals from scientists all over the world, and Olivia Jones, an astronomer at the Royal Observatory in Edinburgh, revealed that some of the early targets will be the Large and Small Magellanic Clouds, two small galaxies at the edge of the Milky Way. Jones will be involved in a dozen different observation campaigns in which the galaxies' chemical composition will be catalogued. Astronomers already know these two galaxies contain a lower metal content than the Milky Way, suggesting a different chemical evolution. Jones also noted that the telescope will focus on the Butterfly Nebula, the remnant of a giant exploded star approximately 3,800 light years from Earth.

A picture of the Butterfly Nebula taken by the Hubble

Scientists calculate the age of the universe at 13.8 billion years, and while Hubble has come within 500 million years of that, but it is hoped that Webb will decrease that number to view the first galaxies a generation earlier. Between first and second-generation galaxies, there lies a tremendous difference in development. In the beginning, gravity had already condensed gas into the first stars, producing the "heavy elements"[134] of carbon and oxygen. In the second generation, stars collected this rich gas as gravity began to group them.

Scientists also hope that Webb will solve the riddle of dark matter by revealing the degree of evidence for it in the early eons of the universe. As far back as 10 billion years, galaxies were far more chaotic than in the present. There was much more activity among supernovae and 10 times more star formation, including "more mergers between galaxies."[135] The decline is difficult to explain, and it is hoped that Webb's spectrographic instruments can determine the answer. In the process of merging galaxies, the theory of a huge early star collapse forming the first black holes will be tested. The opposite may also prove to be true, as the stars theoretically pulled together first through gravitational attraction, causing central black holes to form later.

In a study of the life cycle of stars, Webb's ability to observe the mid-infrared portion of the light spectrum should allow astronomers to view planet formation in the dusty protoplanetary discs that block visible light. The "brown dwarf" is a "specific mystery"[136] to which

[134] Webb Telescope.org, Early Universe, The Beginning of Everything – www.webbtelescope.org/webb-science/early-universe

[135] Webb Telescope.org, Curiosity – www/webbtelescope.org/webb-science/other-worlds

[136] Webb Telescope, Curiosity

scientists hope to address, because the brown dwarf contains properties of both planets and stars. It can host an atmosphere with thick clouds but possesses a mass many times that of Jupiter. They are not massive enough to generate their own light, but some are found in binary relationships with other stars.

Webb is perfectly suited for the task. It is reportedly so powerful that it could "detect the heat of a bumblebee as far away as the Moon."[137] Its detection capabilities surpass those of Hubble by 100 times, and in an interview for *60 Minutes*, astrophysicist Amber Straughn explained, "It's like we have this 14-billion-year-old story of the universe, but we're missing the first chapter."[138] That can only be solved by reaching back 100 million years or more before Hubble.

The need for infrared capability is confirmed by the alternate sight of COBE and WMAP satellites. The two detected microwaves and heat signatures left by the Big Bang 380,000 years after its occurrence, and at that point, there were no stars or galaxies. After the Big Bang, the universe was like "a hot soup of particles such as protons, neutrons, and electrons"[139] that eventually began to combine into ionized atoms of hydrogen and some

[137] Sophie Lewis, CBS News, The James Webb Telescope is So Powerful, It Can Detect the Heat of a Bumblebee as Far Away as the Moon – and Other Surprising Facts, January 25, 2022 – www.cbsnews.com/news/james-webb-space-telescope-fun-facts/

[138] Sophie Lewis

[139] JWST.NASA.gov/James Webb Space Telescope, Goddard Flight Center – www.jwst.nasa.gov/content/science/firstLight

helium. Attracting electrons, they were turned into "neutral atoms,"[140] thereby allowing light to travel freely for the first time.

In the instant after the Big Bang, the universe consisted of "radiation, hydrogen, helium, and high energy particles at a temperature of 18 billion degrees Fahrenheit…400,000 years later, it had cooled to 5,500 degrees, and the universe was glowing a dull red."[141] A few hundred million years passed before the first sources of light were formed, "ending the cosmic dark ages."[142] By the time light reaches Earth from 13.6 billion years in the past, its color or wavelength has stretched to red, called a "redshift"[143] due to universal expansion. This means that light emitted by the first stars beginning in the "visible and ultraviolent spectrums actually gets shifted to redder wavelengths by the time we see it here and now."[144] For very high redshifts (the farthest objects), visible light shifts into the Near and Mid-Infrared part of the electromagnetic spectrum.

After "ultra-deep near-infrared surveys"[145] of the universe, Webb will follow up with "low-resolution spectroscopy and mid-infrared photometry, the

---

[140] JWST.NASA.gov

[141] Chris Holt

[142] JWST.NASA.gov

[143] JWST.NASA.gov

[144] JWST.NASA.gov

[145] JWST.NASA.gov

measurement of the intensity of an astronomical object's electromagnetic radiation."[146]

The process of particles pairing up is known as "Recombination."[147] The period of recombination occurred between 240,000 and 300,000 years after the Big Bang. During this time, the universe went from "opaque to transparent."[148] The period of recombination is "the earliest point in cosmic history"[149] to which scientists can look back with any form of light. Before that, they were in the "dark ages," a period after the universe became transparent but before the first stars were formed.

Theories hold that the first stars were 300 times as massive as the Sun, and millions of times as bright, "burning for only a few million years before exploding as supernovae."[150] If so, these first sources of light may have acted as "seeds for the formation of larger objects."[151] Original supernovae may have collapsed to form the first black holes, and they in turn began to devour gas and other stars to become objects known as "mini-quasars."[152] These grew and merged to become the large black holes present across the universe today.

[146] JWST.NASA.gov
[147] JWST.NASA.gov
[148] JWST.NASA.gov
[149] JWST.NASA.gov
[150] JWST.NASA.gov
[151] JWST.NASA.org
[152] JWST.NASA.org

Stars are the "essential sources of raw materials in the universe, recycling and redistributing the elemental building blocks of everything we observe."[153] That includes "new stars, nebulas of gas and dust, planets, and even humans."[154] All life on Earth contains carbon, "and carbon was formed in the core of a star."[155] Their life cycle proceeds endlessly through "formation, burning fuel, and dispersal of material when the fuel is used up."[156] A star's mass depends on "how much hydrogen is brought together by gravity during its formation."[157] When high-mass stars (those with five times or more mass than the Sun) expend their fuel, their cores begin to collapse "until the pressure overcomes the inward push of gravity."[158] They explode in a spectacular supernova, after which they can go one of two ways. If the remnant is less than three times the mass of the Sun, it will collapse into a "small, very dense core of neutrons called a neutron star."[159] If the remnant is larger than three times the Sun's mass, gravity overwhelms the neutrons and the star collapses completely into a black hole.

These unanswered questions take astronomers back to the beginning and remains for Webb to potentially solve.

[153] Webbtelescope.org, Our Study of the Universe Started with Stargazing – www.webbtelescope.org/webb-science/the-star-lifecycle

[154] Webbtelescope.org

[155] Webbtelescope.org

[156] Webbtelescope.org

[157] Webbtelescope.org

[158] Webbtelescope.org

[159] Webbtelescope.org

Every cycle has a starting point, so how did the first stars form in the absence of a supernova? How much did the first stars deviate from the life cycles scientists are familiar with today? What role did black holes play? The ESA maintains that exploring the life cycles of stars will be one of Webb's "most significant forthcoming tasks."[160]

Many simple elements are "transformed"[161] into heavier elements during the lifetimes of certain stars "which then spread these heavier elements further into space."[162] They are dispersed through stellar winds and supernovae explosions. These explosions will become a primary subject of Webb's work, as they are "the most energetic events in the cosmos and carry information about the death of a star.

The Cosmic Evolution Early Release Science Survey, led by Steven L. Finkelstein of the University of Texas Austin, will be one of the first teams to employ Webb. Over 60 hours of observation time will be spent searching a piece of the sky known as the Extended Growth Strip. Their study will serve as an extension of earlier Hubble research in the Cosmic Assembly Near-Infrared Deep Extragalactic Legacy Survey. Many data points exist for the early universe, but not enough to create "an exhaustive

---

[160] Republic World, Webb Telescope Will Unravel Mysteries of Collapsing Stars and Exoplanets; ESA Explains How – www.republicsorld.com/technology-news/webb-telescope-will-unravel-mysteries-of-collapsing-stars-and-exoplanets-esa-explains-how.html

[161] Republic World

[162] Republic World

census of its conditions."[163] The universe was far more compact in its early development, and "stars and galaxies could have formed at greater efficiency."[164] Finkelstein suggests that some predict "we will find 50 galaxies at the earliest eras, but others predict we will find only a few."[165]

Remaining questions for Webb include the confirmation of what was responsible for converting the gas from neutral to ionized, and how long it took "before the universe became significantly less opaque and much more transparent. Where the new galaxies appear in the sky will offer a clue as to how isolated they were."[166] The prospects are tantalizing to scientists: "We'll open the spectrograph's micro-shutter slits to individually observe hundreds of galaxies to obtain spectra for the first time."[167]

In a study of the "mysterious aspects"[168] of comets, four themes are pursued. The first is cometary activity, followed by comet nucleus heterogeneity, water and ice within comets and on the surfaces, and activity in faint comets and main belt asteroids. Webb will make distinct detections of gas, especially carbon dioxide.

The main asteroid belt and the Trojan belt are all

[163] Claire Bloom, Space Telescope Science Institute, Baltimore, MD, June 25, 2020 –
www.Nasa.gov/feature/goddard/2020/mapping-the-early-universe-with-james-webb-telescope
[164] Claire Bloom
[165] Claire Bloom
[166] Claire Bloom
[167] Claire Bloom
[168] Cometary Science with the James Webb Space Telescope, Astronomical Society of the Pacific –
www.jstor.reed.edu/stable/26659919

observable at some point within the telescope's lifespan. The study of asteroids covers wavelength regions "unavailable from the ground with unprecedented sensitivity."[169] The instrument's spectrograph will investigate multiple planetary atmospheres to determine their atomic and molecular composition, to probe their vertical and horizontal structure, and to follow their dynamic evolution, including "exoplanet weather."[170]

The Main Asteroid Belt is located between the orbits of Mars and Jupiter and is thought to contain millions of objects, but thus far, "only tens of thousands have been observed."[171] It is sparsely populated, and distribution is not uniform. Areas where there are almost no asteroids are known as the "Kirkwood gaps."[172] A Trojan asteroid is distinguished from a Main Belt asteroid because the Trojan "crosses Earth's orbit."[173]

The study of comets is a high priority. Webb operates from 5 to 28.5 pm in the infrared and combines over this range an unprecedented sensitivity level, "a subarc second angular resolution, freedom from atmospheric interference, and the inherent ability of observing in space."[174] In addition to these sizeable advantages, the

[169] Asteroids and the James Webb Space Telescope, Astronomical Society of the Pacific, Vol. 126, No. 946 (December 2014)

[170] Observations of Transiting Exoplanets with the James Webb Space Telescope (JWST), Astronomical Society of the Pacific, Vol. 126, No. 946 (December 2014)

[171] Cosmos, Main Asteroid Belt – www.astronomy.swin.edu/au/M/Main+Asteroid+Belt

[172] Cosmos

[173] Eclipse Aviation, What Distinguishes a Trojan Asteroid from Belt Asteroids – www.eclipseaviation.com/what-distinguishes-trojan-asteroids-from-belt-asteroids

telescope possesses "a suite of versatile capabilities"[175] including low to medium-restoration spectroscopy.

Webb will study three types of comets. Astronomers are already familiar with the first two, Read and Borrelly. Read is a Jupiter-Family comet, while Borrelly is a Main Belt Comet orbiting within the Asteroid Belt. The third is described as a "Target of Opportunity."[176] Scientists hope to discover a suitable candidate within the first year of operation. If fortunate, "they will capture an interstellar comet"[177] or train Webb upon a comet from the Oort Cloud, a spherical cloud surrounding our solar system. Comets have changed little in the solar system's 4.6-billion-year history and are among the most ancient bodies available for study.

Heidi Hammel, planetary scientist selected as a Webb Disciplinary Scientist in 2002, will serve as part of NASA's Webb Guaranteed Observation Time team. She will be among the first to demonstrate Webb's capacities for tracking and viewing bright objects.

Molecules of gas and dust emit infrared wavelengths of light, so Webb can determine which chemicals are present. Among the themes to be emphasized in cometary

---

[174] Eclipse Aviation

[175] The Mid-Infrared Instrument for the James Webb Space Telescope, I: Introduction, *Astronomical Society of the Pacific*, Vol. 124 No. 953 (July 2015)

[176] Webbtelescope.org, Nasa's Webb to Unlock the Mysteries of Comets and the Early Solar System, Sept. 25, 2019 – www.telescope.org/contents/news-releases/2019/news-2019-45

[177] Webbtelescope.org

science for Webb are cot nucleus heterogeneity, water ice in comae and on the surface, and activity in faint comets.

The large aperture of Webb, combined with the Near-Infrared and Mid-Infrared instruments will make the telescope capable of studying comet gas, dust, and nuclei at "moderate and large heliocentric distances."[178] Operation strategies allow us to follow comets over a wide range of times and distance.

This study should help with present questions pertaining to "initial stages of the solar system foundation and subsequent evolution."[179] Primordial sources of organic matter and the "nature of interstellar matter that was incorporated"[180] is a subject of great interest. Webb should also help to answer where organic synthesis continues today, and how have the myriad chemical and physical processes that shape the solar system operated, interacted, and evolved over time."[181]

Over the past three decades, more than 5,000 exoplanets have been discovered. They cover a vast range of sizes, masses, and temperatures. Orbiting all kinds of stars, the planets held in gravitational check range from "small, rocky exoplanets to giant gaseous ones."[182] Webb will

---

[178] Iopscience, Cometary Science with the James Webb Telescope – www.iopscience.org/article/10.1088/1538-3873/128/959/018009

[179] Iopscience

[180] Iopscience

[181] Iopscience

[182] Scitech Daily, Webb Space Telescope Will Study Formation, Composition, Clouds of Distant Worlds, Goddard Space Flight

observe them by employing a "transit technique."[183] Observation data will be collected over the course of a planet's orbit to enable measurements of atmospheric composition and dynamics.

The first year calls for a regimen of studying small exoplanets orbiting stars smaller and cooler than the Sun, known as "M Dwarfs."[184] They have only been discovered in the last few years, and Webb will search for water molecules, carbon dioxide, and methane in their atmospheres. M-Dwarfs are more active than the Sun and have "energetic stellar flares,"[185] which may reveal that the exoplanets have no atmosphere at all.

For the vast majority of discovered exoplanets, knowledge is "indirect."[186] Scientists can usually only see them as points of light, but in recent years some have been "direct imaged."[187] Exoplanets are usually close to much brighter stars, so their light "is generally overwhelmed by the light of the host star."[188] Usually, their presence is only detected as they pass across the front of their star, called a "transit."[189] At times, the gravitational attraction

---

Center, April 15, 2022 – www.scitechdaily.com/webb-space-telescope-will-study-formation-composition-clouds-of-distant-worlds/

[183] Scitech Daily

[184] Scitech Daily

[185] Scitech Daily

[186] Ann Jenkins, Space Telescope Institute, Baltimore, MD, A New View of Exoplanets with NASA's Upcoming Webb Telescope – www.nasa.gov/feature/goddard/2019/a-new-view-of-exoplanets-with-nasa-s-webb-telescope

[187] Ann Jenkins

[188] Ann Jenkins

[189] Ann Jenkins

of a planet tugs on a star, causing it to wobble slightly.

At other times, coronagraphs can be used to block the glare from a host star. This is a difficult process, but Webb has a coronagraph onboard. Related to eclipses, these instruments act as an "artificial eclipse."[190] Most planets detected so far are roughly 10,000-1,000,000 times fainter than the host star. With Webb, astronomers can see planets up to 100 million times fainter.

Time with the telescope will be granted immediately to exoplanetary researchers as part of the Director's Discretionary Early Release Science program. The fortunate team will employ all four of Webb's instruments to observe three targets – a recently discovered exoplanet, an object that is either an exoplanet or a "brown dwarf," and a well-studied ring of dust and planetesimals orbiting a young star.

The exoplanet, newly discovered, has a mass between six and 12 times that of Jupiter, and it orbits a star twice as massive as the Sun. It resides roughly 92 times farther from its star as Earth does to its Sun. The planetary mass at the "planet/dwarf boundary"[191] is also widely separated from its star. The debris disk (rings) around the young star HR4796A has twice the mass of the Sun. Webb's goal is to see if structures of the disk look different from

---

190 Ann Jenkins

191 Ann Jenkins

wavelength to wavelength.

At first glance, viewing disturbance of soil on exoplanets might seem like an outlandish theory in the search for extraterrestrial life, but Webb can likely view the phenomenon if it exists. One of the key developments of separating modern civilization from hunter gatherer societies of the past is the invention of farming around 10,000 years ago. Scientists figure that examples of such activity should be visible from space as "exo-farms."[192] Nitrogen in the soil can be detected, or ammonia in the atmosphere from nitrogen fertilizers. Odd as it may seem, this has been added to the catalogue of "extraterrestrial technosignatures."[193]

Titan, one of Saturn's moons, is a priority for telescope, and a unique regimen of spectroscopy and imaging of Mars will also be conducted. The water ratio of Mars will be mapped, and the Martian mesosphere will be studied, including dust and water-ice clouds. Simultaneously, the telescope will conduct "sensitive searches for trace species and hydrated features on the Martian surface."[194]

The Titan project will be part of a general study of Saturn, its rings, and its family of moons. This study will begin almost immediately during the first observation

---

[192] Discover, Evidence of Farming on Exoplanets Should be Visible to the James Webb Telescope –
   www.discovermagazine.com/the-sciences/evidence-of-farming-on-exoplanets-should-be-visible-to-the-james-webb
[193] Discover
[194] Michael Turner

phase and comprise a "comprehensive solar system program."[195] Webb will also pick up where Cassini left off after orbiting Saturn for 13 years. Five core science themes will be in play for Titan. The first is the surface, followed by tropospheric clouds. Next comes tropospheric gases, stratospheric composition, and stratospheric hazes.

Saturn experiences seasons as it orbits the Sun. The Saturnian year is 30 Earth years long, with each season lasting 7.5 years. Cassini arrived during the southern hemisphere's summer, and astronomers are eager to witness season changes. In 2010, a monster storm erupted on Saturn's surface, and by January 2011, had encircled the entire planet. Other atmospheric phenomena viewed by Webb will include auroras, northern and southern lights. They trigger chemical changes in Saturn's atmosphere.

Titan is the only moon in the solar system with a "substantial atmosphere."[196] It is larger than the planet Mercury, and the atmospheric pressure is 50% greater than it is on Earth. Like Earth, the atmosphere is comprised mostly of nitrogen, but it also has vaporous hydrocarbons like methane. Temperatures are far colder than on Earth, plunging to -290 degrees Fahrenheit.

Conor Nixon of the Goddard Space Flight Center is a

---

[195] Christine Pulliam
[196] Christine Pulliam

principal scientist for the study of Titan, and as he put it,
"Titan's atmosphere is like a big chemistry lab."[197] It is
also the only other known body in the solar system with
liquid seas and lakes on the surface. Stefanie Milam of
Goddard explained, "Titan has clouds and weather that we
can see changing in real time. Its chemistry is very
different from Earth's, but it's still organic, carbon-based
chemistry."[198]

The Future

The telescope's estimated usage is expected to last
between five and 12 years, but it could last longer. NASA
has accredited an increase in the expected lifespan of the
telescope to the successful launch and efficiency in space,
"which resulted in less propellant usage." Ever since the
telescope was ejected from the Ariane 5 rocket's first
stage booster, "it is moving on its own using its own fuel."[199]
In the simplest of explanations, "more propellant means
more science."[200] The launch was more precise than
anticipated, and "exceeded the requirements needed to put
Webb on the right path."[201] Little fuel or effort was
expended in the deployment of the telescope solar array.
Propellant tanks were filled with 79.5 liters of extremely
toxic dinitrogen tetroxide.

---

[197] Christine Pulliam

[198] Christine Pulliam

[199] Harsh Vardhan

[200] Republic World

[201] Republic World

Either way, it is hoped that the telescope can watch Saturn moving from northern summer through the autumnal equinox back to the southern spring. That would represent, including Cassini's time, the potential completion of a Saturnian year. Webb will pay particular attention to the "saturation"[202] of the instruments with moisture, but the problem may be alleviated by quicker read-out times.

A study of Near-Earth Objects (NEOs) will be catalogued over the first two years. Over 75% of NEOs can be observed in any given year, but James Webb Space Telescope will need to wait for observation windows. The telescope can easily execute "photometric observations of meter-sized NEOs."[203] In the search for planetary rings and small satellites, James Webb Space Telescope will attempt to discover new rings and moons, conduct an unprecedented degree of spectroscopy, and make time-domain observations.

The Webb observatory is comprised of three elements, including the Integrated Science Instrument Module (ISIM). The Optical Telescope Element (OTE) includes the backplane of the mirrors and Spacecraft Element. This includes the Spacecraft bus and sunshield. The Science Instrument Module houses the cameras and all science

---

[202] NTRS, NASA Technical Reports Server, Titan Science with the James Webb Space Telescope –
www.ntrs.nasa.gov/citations/20170006874

[203] Michael Turner

instruments. These will have to function in perfectly synchronized fashion in order to study NEOs.

A new paper by a planetary researcher Vishnu Reddy has been published explaining how Webb will allow scientists to better study and understand Near-Earth Objects. NEOs, asteroids, and comets whose orbits bring them close to Earth's are "tracked to determine potentially destructive collisions with Earth."[204]

NEOs are also seen as a "possible source of water and other materials needed to allow human-tended space missions to distant worlds."[205] From its orbital position, James Webb Space Telescope could have access to "observe nearly three-quarters of all NEOs, and nearly all asteroids and comets beyond Mars."[206] Webb has strict requirements "for pointing, which could be problematic for the fastest moving NEOs,"[207] but 75% of them meet the observability requirements.

Photometric observations of small particles are possible. Asteroid and NEO analysis will be available for surface composition and "characterization of absorption and emission features."[208] Imaging in Near-Infrared at V Band

---

[204] Phys.org, James Webb Space Telescope to offer better view of Near-Earth Objects, Planetary Science Institute. Feb. 9, 2016 – www.phys.org/2016-02-james-webb-space-telescope-view.html

[205] Phys.org

[206] Phys.org

[207] Phys.org

[208] Stsci.edu, James Webb Space Telescope, Asteroids and Near-Earth Objects – www.stci.edu/files/live/sites/home/jwst/about/history/flyers/_documents/JWST-Asteroids.pdf.

will offer an unprecedented study of "surface heterogeneity, and of shapes, dust, outgassing, and multiplicity."[209] Imaging and Spectroscopy will "enable a detailed study of albedos, sizes, surface roughness, and thermal inertia."[210] Albedo is "the proportion of the incident light that is reflected by a surface."[211] Thermal inertia is best explained as "the measure of responsiveness of material to variations in temperature."[212]

Meanwhile, NASA is accelerating its work on the development of space telescopes, contemplating Webb's successor despite the fact the telescope only recently reached space. The agency is reportedly "exploring the possibility of creating liquid lenses to make a gigantic telescope, perhaps 100 times the size of the Webb."[213] The theory began as a strictly theoretical question but is already part way through a series of experiments to see if fluids can be used to create "lenses in microgravity."[214] Liquid lenses would be less useful than optical lenses in Earth's gravity, but "they excel at focusing light"[215] in that environment.

Regardless, the increase in Webb's resolution must be

---

[209] Stsci.edu

[210] Stsci.edu

[211] Merriam-Webster – www.Merriam-Webster.com/dictionary/albedo

[212] Encyclopedia.com, Thermal Inertia – www.encyclopedia.com

[213] Michael Zhang, NASA Liquid Lens Space Telescope Could be 100 Times the Size of Webb, April 6, 2022 – www.petapixal.com/2022/or/06/nasa-liquid-lens-telescope-could-be-100-times-the-size-of-webb/

[214] Michael Zhang

[215] Michael Zhang

considered a significant human achievement. Its optical resolution sits at 0.1 seconds, and its wavelength coverage at 0.6 to 28.5 microns has never been approached. Even Webb's first test photo is "the highest resolution image ever taken from space."[216] Webb is currently demonstrating "unprecedented resolution."[217] Put simply, astronomers already marvel at its clarity: "The sensitive gains and the image clarity will both be a factor of 100 better than ever before."[218] With that, startling cosmic revelations are anticipated.

· ·

Online Resources

Other books about space by Charles River Editors

Other books about the universe on Amazon

Further Reading

Asteroids and the James Webb Space Telescope, Astronomical Society of the Pacific – www.jstor.reed.edu/stable/266559913

Ball.com, Webb Space Telescope –

[216] Interesting Engineering, James Webb Space Telescope's Infrared Sensors Will Mark a Major Step in Astronomy – www.interestingengineering.com/james-webb-telescope-infrared

[217] Interesting Engineering

[218] Interesting Engineering

www.ball.com/aerospace/programs/astrophysics/webb

Big Think, 10 Unbelievable but True Facts about NASA's James Webb Space Telescope – www.bigthink.com/starts-with-a-bang/to-facts-james-webb

Blogs.NASA, James Webb Space Telescope, Webb's Cool View on How Stars, Planets Form – www.blogs.nasa.gov/webb/2022/04/07/webbs-cool-view-on-how-stars-and-planets-form/

Bloom, Claire, Space Telescope Science Institute, Baltimore, MD, June 25, 2020 – www.Nasa.gov/feature/goddard/2020/mapping-the-early-universe-with-james-webb-telescope

\Boston Micromachines Corporation, Perform at a Higher Level with the Latest Technology – www.bostonmicromachines.com/deformablemirror-applications/astronomy/

Britannica.com, Envision the birth of stars and planets illuminated through the infrared eye of the James Webb Space Telescope – www.britannica.com/video/154216/James-Webb-Space-Telescope-stars

Bryan, Victoria, NASA delays launch of Webb telescope after preparation incident –

www.aerotime.aero/articles/129522-nasa-delays-launch-of-webb-telescope

Cometary Science with the James Webb Space Telescope, Astronomical Society of the Pacific – www.jstor.reed.edu/stable/26659919

Cosmos Magazine Newsletter, What's the James Webb Space Telescope Up to Now? – www.cosmosmagazine.com/space/astronomy/james-webb-space-telescope-cooling

Cosmos, Main Asteroid Belt – www.astronomy.swin.edu/au/M/Main+Asteroid+Belt

Devlin, Scott, Harwood, Mark, What You Need to Know About the James Webb Space Telescope, Creation.com/Dec. 26, 2021 – www.creation.com/the-famous-webb-space-telescope

Discover, Evidence of Farming on Exoplanets Should be Visible to the James Webb Telescope – www.discovermagazine.com/the-sciences/evidence-of-farming-on-exoplanets-should-be-visible-to-the-james-webb

Eclipse Aviation, What Distinguishes a Trojan Asteroid from Belt Asteroids – www.eclipseaviation.com/what-distinguishes-trojan-asteroids-from-belt-asteroids

Encyclopedia.com, Thermal Inertia – www.encyclopedia.com

Ferguson, William, WSU Insider, WSU Physicist to Study Black Holes with the James Webb Telescope, Dec. 7, 2021 – www.wsu.edu/press-release/2021/12/07

Goddard Space Flight Center, James Webb Space Telescope – www.James Webb Space Telescope.nasa.gov

Goddard Flight Center, James Webb Space Telescope, Infrared Detectors – www.James Webb Space Telescope.nasa.gov/content/about/innovations/infrared.html

Go Photonics, Harris Corporation to Test James Webb Space Telescope for NASA – www.gophotonics.com/details/797/harris-corporation-to-test-james-webb-space-telescope-for-nasa

Harwood, William, NASA's Webb Telescope achieves near-perfect focus, whetting appetites for discoveries to come, CBS News, March 16, 2022 – www.cbsnews.com/news/nasa-webb-telescope-near-perfect-focus/

Holt, Chris, How the James Webb Telescope will Peer Back in Time, April 5, 2022, Discover – www.DiscoverMagazine.com/the-sciences/how-the-james-webb-telescope-will-peer-back-in-time

Innotech Today, An Inside Look at Cryocooler Tech for the James Webb Telescope – www.innotechtoday.com/an-inside-llok-at-cryocooler-tech-fir-the-james-webb-telescope

Iopscience, Cometary Science with the James Webb Telescope – www.iopscience.org/article/10.1088/1538-3873/128/959/018009

Interesting Engineering, James Webb Space Telescope's Infrared Sensors Will Mark a Major Step in Astronomy – www.interestingengineering.com/james-webb-telescope-infrared

James E. Webb, NASA Administrator, Feb. 14, 1961, October 7, 1968 – www.history.nasa.gov/biographical/webb.html

Jenkins, Ann, Space Telescope Institute, Baltimore, MD, A New View of Exoplanets with NASA's Upcoming Webb Telescope – www.nasa.gov/feature/goddard/2019/a-new-view-of-exoplanets-with-nasa-s-webb-telescope

James Webb Space Telescope.NASA.gov/James Webb Space Telescope, Goddard Flight Center – www.James Webb Space Telescope.nasa.gov/content/science/firstLight

Lewis Sophie, CBS News, The James Webb is so powerful, it can detect the heat of a bumblebee as far away as the moon – and other surprising facts, Jan. 25, 2022 – www.cbsnews.com/james-webb-space-telescope-fun-facts/

Lockheed Martin, James Webb Space Telescope's Powerful Eyes – www.lockheedmartin.com/3n-us/news/features/2021/NIRCam-see-universe-in-new-light.html

May, Andrew, James Webb Space Telescope: Origins, Design, and Mission Objectives, March, 2022, Live Science – www.livescience.com/james-webb-space-telescope

Merriam-Webster – www.Merriam-Webster.com/dictionary/albedo

NASA, James Webb Space Telescope – www.nasa.gov/mission_pages/Webb/team/index.html

NASA.gov/ Our Cosmic Time Machine. The James Webb Space Telescope, Oct. 6, 2020 – www.nasa.gov/mediacast/our-cosmic-time-machine-the-james-webb-space-telescope

NASA.gov, Goddard, NASA's Webb will Join Forces with the Event Horizon Telescope to Reveal the Milky Way's Supermassive Black Hole –

www.nasa.gov/feature/goddard/2021/nasa-s-webb-will-
join-forces-with-the-event-horizon-telescope-to-reveal-
the-milky-way-supermassive-black-hole

News.Yahoo.com, A New Window on the Universe is
about to Open Wide: Excitement Building at Baltimore
Institute for the James Webb Space Telescope's
Observations – www.news.yahoo.com/window-universe-
open-wide-excitement-090000710.html

Northrop Grumman, James Webb Space Telescope –
www.northropgrumman.com/space/james-webb-space-
telescope/

Observations of Transiting Exoplanets with the James
Webb Space Telescope (James Webb Space Telescope),
Astronomical Society of the Pacific, Vol. 126, No. 946
(December 2014)

Phy.org, James Webb Space Telescope to offer better
view of Near-Earth Objects, Planetary Science Institute.
Feb. 9, 2016 – www.phys.org/2016-02-james-webb-
space-telescope-view.html

Pulliam, Christine, Space Telescope Institute, Baltimore,
MD, How to Weight a Black Hole Using NASA's Webb
Space Telescope –
www.nasa.gov/feature/goddard/2018/how-to-weigh-a-
black-hole-using-nasa-s-webb-space-telescope

Republic World, Webb Telescope Will Unravel
Mysteries of Collapsing Stars and Exoplanets; ESA
Explains How – www.republicsorld.com/technology-
news/webb-telescope-will-unravel-mysteries-of-
collapsing-stars-and-exoplanets-esa-explains-how.html

Science and Exploration, L@, The Second Lagrangian
Point –
www.esa.int/Science_Exploration/Space_Science/L2_the
_second_Lagrangian_Point

Scientific American, New Revelations Pressure on
NASA to Rename the James Webb Space Telescope –
www.scientificamerican.com/article/new-revelations-
raise-pressure-on-nasa-to-rename-the-james-webb-space-
telescope/

Scientific Visualization Studio, NASA, James Webb
Telescope – www.gsfc.gov/Gallery/James Webb Space
Telescope.html

Scitech Daily, Webb Space Telescope will Study
Formation, Composition, Clouds of Distant Worlds,
Goddard Space Flight Center, April 15, 2022 –
www.scitechdaily.com/webb-space-telescope-will-study-
formation-composition-clouds-of-distant-worlds/

Solar System Science, Nasa.gov, Overview of Titan –
www.solarsystem.nasa.gov/moons/saturn-

moons/titan/overview/

Space Versus Ground Telescopes, June 7, 2016, University of Arizona – www.research.arizona.edu/stories/space-versus-ground-telescopes

Stsci.edu, James Webb Space Telescope, Asteroids and Near-Earth Objects – www.stci.edu/files/live/sites/home/James Webb Space Telescope/about/history/flyers/_documents/James Webb Space Telescope-Asteroids.pdf.

Strickland, Ashley, Webb Telescope's first test images include an unexpected 'selfie', CNN – www.cnn.com/2022/02/11/world/james-webb-space-telescope-selfie-images-scn/index.html

Sutherland, Paige, Skoog, Tom. Chakrabarti, Meghna, The Remarkable Story of the James Webb Space Telescope – www.wbur.org/2022/04/01/masa-space-story-of-the-james-webb-space-telescope

The Mid-Infrared Instrument for the James Webb Space Telescope, I: Introduction, Astronomical Society of the Pacific, Vol. 127 No. 953 (July 2015)

Turner, Michael, Much More Than a Telescope, Science, JSTOR, Reed College

UNews@the U, NASA's Webb Telescope will help unlock secrets of black holes – www.nasa.miam.edu/stories/2022/01/nasa-webb-telescope-will-help-unlock-secrets-of-black-holes.html

Vardhan, Harsh, Republic World, NASA Confirms James Webb Telescope Will Last Longer than 10 Years – www.republicworld.com/science/space/nasa/nasa-confirms-james-webb-space-telescope-will-last-longer-than-expected-10-yr-lifespan-articleshow.html

Webb Space Telescope, James Webb Telescope Overview, University of Arizona – www.James Webb Space Telescope.arizona.edu/mission

Webb Telescope.org, Early Universe, The Beginning of Everything – www.webbtelescope.org/webb-science/early-universe

Webb Telescope.org, Curiosity – www.webbtelescope.org/webb-science/other-worlds

Webbtelescope.org, NASA's Webb to Unlock the Mysteries of Comets and the Early Solar System, Sept. 25, 2019 – www.telescope.org/contents/news-releases/2019/news-2019-45

Webbtelescope.org, Our Study of the Universe Started with Stargazing – www.webbtelescope.org/webb-science/the-star-lifecycle

Zhang, Michael, NASA Liquid Lens Space Telescope Could be 100 Times the Size of Webb, April 6, 2022 – www.petapixel.com/2022/04/06/nasa-liquid-lens-space-telescope-could-be-100-times-the-size-of-webb/

Free Books by Charles River Editors

We have brand new titles available for free most days of the week. To see which of our titles are currently free, click on this link.

Discounted Books by Charles River Editors

We have titles at a discount price of just 99 cents everyday. To see which of our titles are currently 99 cents, click on this link.